The Traveller's
Guide to
Sovereign Hill

ISBN 0-909874-21-2

Produced and published by
The Sovereign Hill Museums Association
ACN 004 688 733
Sovereign Hill Post Office,
Ballarat, Victoria, Australia 3350.
Telephone 03 5331 1944
Facsimile 03 5331 1528

Editor: Helen Smithers
Art Director: John Zulic
Design: Glenn Bishop
Photography: Daryl Hunt
Additional Photographs: Tim Scanlon, Michael McLeod,
Bill McAuley, Ian Roberts, Gary Edwards, Tourism Victoria

Our Photographs

*For the photographs in this guide book, our staff and
volunteers have put aside their daily routine, for a few
moments, to pose in the manner favoured by the mid-
Victorian outdoor photographers who captured many
wonderful images of Australia's goldfields. We have used this
style of photography to place our buildings and costumed
characters within their historical context.*

Contents

Welcome to
Sovereign Hill

WHO WE ARE...

Sovereign Hill is an Outdoor Museum which captures the impact of the Gold Rush on Ballarat, with particular emphasis upon the first decade, from 1851. Sovereign Hill attracts over 550,000 visitors annually and enjoys international recognition as a living museum, with a heavy emphasis on working machinery and exhibits, costumed interpreters and visitor participation.

The Sovereign Hill Museums Association, which administers Sovereign Hill, is a non-profit community-based organisation, structured as a company limited by guarantee. The Association is controlled by a Board who are elected by Members and serve voluntarily. Membership of the Association is open to all. Management is in the hands of an Executive Director and professional staff. In all, some 350 people are employed.

WHAT WE ARE ABOUT...

For many Australians, the name Ballarat is a link with one of the most exciting periods in our history – the Gold Rush era – and its profound effect on our nation. Paradoxically, Ballarat is an aboriginal word meaning "resting place".

Sovereign Hill, therefore, offers a perspective on a great story in Australian history. This representation of Ballarat in its rip-roaring days tells a tale of ordinary people and their efforts to make a better life for themselves during the 1850s Gold Rush.

In August 1851, gold was discovered at Poverty Point, a stone's throw from today's Sovereign Hill. Soon, what had been a peaceful, green valley echoed to the discordant sounds of a gold rush. Trees were felled, acres of ground were stripped and clear streams ran yellow with mud as thousands of fortune-hunters flocked to Ballarat from across the world. Lured by the promise of prosperity few could normally achieve, Ballarat's diggers carved out a rough-and-ready and defiantly independent community.

As mining became established, men brought their families to Ballarat. Tents and humpies were traded for weatherboard cottages and villas, and the community became more settled. Goods from all over the world flooded in to fill shops and to satisfy the townsfolk's demands; advanced technologies of steam, transport and industry were imported and a truly "modern" city emerged.

Although Sovereign Hill is a museum, its story is not told through words and signs alone, and visitors are not herded through a packaged programme of rote-learned commentary. By participating and interacting with our own interpreters, visitors form their own view of the past. Giving visitors the freedom to choose their own paths around the outdoor museum, and to participate in a range of activities, is central to the idea of a living history experience. A visit to Sovereign Hill can be more than just a pleasant outing; it can become an intriguing expedition into a living past. We hope you will enjoy your visit, and that you will take away a memorable glimpse of Australia's history.

VOYAGE TO DISCOVERY ORIENTATION CENTRE

Visitors may wander at will through the Outdoor Museum, but there is a definite historical sequence in the presentation. Our Orientation Centre is designed to give an overview of the Outdoor Museum and to provide a context for the three phases of mining which took place in Ballarat – alluvial, deep lead and quartz mining. The Orientation Centre is therefore placed adjacent to the Entrance Building, and we recommend that you start your visit there.

We have called the Orientation Centre *Voyage to Discovery*. It follows the experience of goldrush immigrants travelling to Australia under sail, their arrival in Melbourne or Geelong and the need to outfit themselves for the diggings, and indeed, to choose a destination. Other displays place the Ballarat gold discoveries in the broader context of gold rushes elsewhere in the state and, subsequently, in other parts of Australia. In dioramas and models, the differences between alluvial, deep lead and quartz mining are illustrated, and this is the underlying theme for a 13 minute audio-visual programme, *Golden Days*, which screens in the auditorium. This is an exciting presentation, at the conclusion of which doors automatically open, leading the visitor to the Diggings.

OUTDOOR MUSEUM

As you leave the Orientation Centre and enter the Outdoor Museum, you will find that Sovereign Hill's goldrush story is told across three precincts. We recommend that you begin your visit in the Red Hill Gully Diggings which represent Ballarat's earliest goldrush history, move on to the Township and, finally, visit the Quartz Mine which takes you through to early 20th century mining in Ballarat.

1. RED HILL GULLY DIGGINGS

In the early 1850s, the first diggers – dressed in colourful shirts, cabbage tree hats and moleskin trousers – flocked in thousands along the edges of creeks and streams, searching for alluvial or surface gold. When most of this easy gold had been taken from the surface (often by individuals), men found it easier to work in groups to sink shallow shafts and find the deeper, buried gold. All this is represented on our Diggings. Mining machinery – whims, windlasses, whips, puddling machines and even a Californian pump – stand side-by-side with diggers' tents and huts. You will find some of these dwellings "inhabited" by our costumed volunteers. They will be happy to chat with you about life on the Diggings and to pose for photographs.

At one end of the Diggings is a Chinese Village. In the later 1850s, Chinese diggers were forced to live apart from hostile European miners, under the care of a Chinese Protector. A fully-consecrated temple is a feature of this village.

Behind the Chinese Temple, we have re-created the Red Hill Mine which presents the story of deep lead alluvial mining – the second developmental stage of Ballarat's mining history. As surface gold ran out, miners dug deeper to reach rich hauls of gold hidden in ancient riverbeds known as deep leads. Conditions in these wet, muddy mines were treacherous, and Ballarat became famous for pioneering deep lead mining technology.

Fully-guided tours of the Diggings and a special *Chinese on the Goldfields* tour are available.

2. TOWNSHIP

In Main Street, you can experience the pace and variety of life as it was in prosperous, rollicking Ballarat of the 1850s. Main Street is lined with buildings representative of those constructed by enterprising businessmen of the mid-1850s. They realised that "gold" could also be won by supplying diggers with goods, services and entertainment – and probably with less effort and greater success!

As you enter Main Street, you will be surrounded by the atmosphere of "daily life" in our Township. Listen for the ring of the blacksmith's hammer and the beat of hooves as horses pull a coach or a wagon-load of wool bales up the hill. The inviting aromas of ground coffee and spices waft out from Clarke Brothers' Grocery to greet visitors and mingle with the tang of wood smoke. The Criterion Store will take you back to the graceful world of crinolines and frock-coats. Or, if you visit the "residents" of Speedwell Street, you will find the fascinating details of domestic life as it was carried out in Ballarat's early cottages and villas.

Apart from wonderful shopping and photographic opportunities, many of our businesses and workshops feature talks and demonstrations throughout the day, and our volunteers in the Speedwell Street residences are always happy to greet visitors.

3. Quartz Mine

Atop the massive timber Poppet Head you will see the yellow flag of the Sovereign Quartz Mining Company flying proudly. As you enter the fenced-in area, you leave the 1850s and step into the later period of large quartz mining companies.

Above ground, you can see a re-creation of the surface installations required by large quartz mines. These date from the later part of the 19th century. The great wooden beam of a Cornish Beam Pump rises and sinks, raising water from the mine below. In the Boiler House, the two wood-fired boilers produce steam to power engines which drive the Winder Engine, the Beam Pump and the Battery. This Battery crushes quartz under its thundering stampers so that gold can be extracted from the crushings. The Gold Smelting Works completes the story of gold with the smelting and pouring of a spectacular gold ingot.

Visitors can also join a guided tour of the Underground Mine, walking through tunnels which have been driven through earth beneath the Township. Along these tunnels, displays illustrate mining techniques and conditions typical of Ballarat's quartz mines between 1860 and 1916, when the last mine closed down. You can also walk through fascinating discoveries of actual old workings unearthed during construction of the Mine, for Sovereign Hill stands on the site of a number of historical mines: Normanby North, Speedwell Quartz Mining Company and Llanberris No. 2, for instance.

There is also a special exhibit in the Mine. *The Secret Chamber* is a colourful state-of-the-art presentation which employs dramatic special effects to tell the story of the Chinese on the goldfields. It is available as part of the *Chinese on the Goldfields* tour.

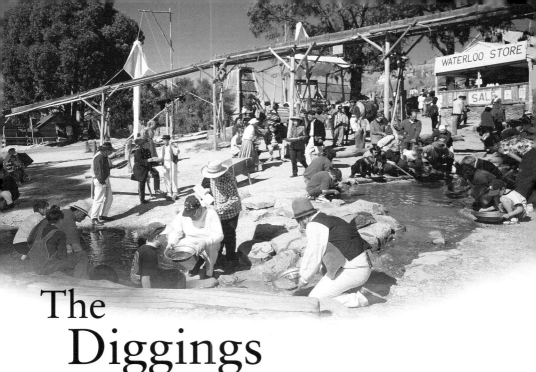

The Diggings

RED HILL GULLY CREEK

In the early 1850s, diggers panned and cradled for gold in the alluvial sands and gravels around creeks and rivers. They were called "alluvial" because the material (including the gold) had been washed down from surrounding hills by erosion.

Soon, as surface gold became scarcer, diggers formed small groups to dig shafts deeper into the sands, seeking alluvial leads. A "lead" (rhyming with "bead") was a buried gold-bearing creek bed. Sovereign Hill's Red Hill Gully Creek is actually on the site of such a shallow alluvial lead – the south channel of the Red Hill Lead – where large amounts of gold were found in the 1850s. Inevitably, these mines soon yielded most of their gold and by the early 1860s, most had been abandoned.

Our creek contains real gold and has been constructed to show both types of early mining. Goldpans and cradles are scattered along the creek for visitors wishing to try their luck. Back from the creek are diggers' tents and huts and the shafts and machinery of shallow alluvial mines.

GOLDPANNING AND CRADLING

Goldpanning was (and still is) the means by which gold prospectors checked creek beds for alluvial gold. A show of gold in creek beds meant that it would probably be found in sand and gravel beside the stream. Some diggers won large amounts of gold by panning, and many more made a reasonable living this way.

A cradle was often used, instead of a pan, to handle a large amount of washdirt. Washdirt was placed in the sieve at the top of the cradle, and water was poured onto it as the cradle was rocked. As clay and gravel washed away, the heavier gold was trapped in the riffles and blankets below the sieve.

WINDLASSES AND WINDSAILS

Experienced diggers realised that gold would also be found in the ground near the creek beds. In small parties of three or four men, they dug shallow shafts into the riverbanks. By using a windlass, the bucket or "kibble" which had been filled with gravel, by a man in the shaft below, could be raised to the surface. The man working the windlass emptied the bucket onto a pile of washdirt. A third miner took barrowloads of this material to the creek where a cradle would be used to separate the gold.

As shafts deepened, conditions for men working below ground got worse, as air quickly became stale, with no circulation. Windsails, which could be turned to catch wind from any direction, were put above the head of the shaft. Air was funnelled down the sails to the men working below. These sails were similar to those used to ventilate below decks on sailing ships.

The shafts in the Diggings have been constructed to show a variety of timbering methods. They are supported by bark and logs, by jointed split timber, round timber, or split timber with wooden pegs. All these methods were used in Ballarat, in the 1850s.

GOLD COMMISSIONER'S CAMP

Our Commissioner's Camp: Our Camp represents the camp as it was in early 1851. At the front of the camp are two tents and a weather shelter. The License Tent contains a simple desk and writing equipment for issuing the compulsory licences for all diggers on the goldfields. The other tent provides space for miners to lodge their gold safely for escort to Melbourne.

A British flag fluttering above reminds miners that, wherever they came from, they are now subject to British law. In fact, the young Colony of Victoria had recently been named after the British Queen of the day. In the absence of a lock-up, chains and leg-irons, fixed to a large log, provide a convenient method of detaining prisoners.

At the rear of the camp, tents provide basic living quarters for troopers. To the right, the Gold Commissioner's tent is more elaborately furnished. A small camp fire allows for basic cooking.

Historical Notes: The Ballarat goldfields were administered by a Government-appointed Commissioner, from the discovery of gold in 1851 until mid-1855. The Gold Commissioner issued licences which cost 30 shillings and permitted miners to dig a claim of 8 feet square per month, after which the licence had to be renewed. Throughout the period of licensing, various conditions changed. In 1854, the fee was equivalent to about a month's earnings for the average digger, and was one of the major grievances which led to the Eureka Stockade uprising in December of that year. After those events, the licence was replaced by a Miner's Right and Gold Commissioners were replaced by Wardens and elected local courts.

DWELLINGS

Around the Diggings, a number of dwellings show the ways in which individuals built homes with what materials they could find in their new surroundings. Some of these dwellings are occupied by costumed volunteers, who go about their daily lives on the Diggings. They are always ready to chat for a while with a visitor – and maybe even share a hot scone.

TENTS

Perhaps the most common form of housing in the early years on the Diggings was the tent. Most began as plain canvas shelters, but they soon became more solid and homely as diggers settled in.

MARRIED COUPLE'S HUT

With mud brick and bark walls and a bark roof secured by bush poles, this hut shows an improvement on the tents and humpies first seen on the goldfields. It has a dirt floor, but the presence of household furniture, the number of beds and the variety of cooking utensils and chinaware indicate some domestic comforts and the presence of a wife and family.

HAMMONDS' HUT

Again, this is a married couple's dwelling, and the presence of a woman is obvious. This digger and his wife will soon need more bed space, but for the moment, their baby sleeps in the bottom drawer of the pine chest! This hut shows another style of roofing – bush poles, suspended from ropes, hold the canvas in place.

SAILORS' HUT

This hut is very basic and seems to be occupied by single men. Two upright logs serve as seats, their beds are the kind of simple canvas bunks seen on ships and their cooking equipment is basic. They seem more concerned with keeping their shovels, ropes, goldpans and cradle safe inside than with domestic comforts.

BUTCHER'S SHAMBLE

A painting called *A Butcher's Shamble, Forest Creek, 1852-3,* by goldfields artist S. T. Gill, was used as the reference for this simple bark "shop" and dwelling.

Our Building: The shamble is typical of the butchers' stalls set up by roadsides to attract passing custom on the early diggings. The diggers' choice was very limited. Meat hung from a pole and the butcher's tools of trade were very simple – a couple of tree stumps (used as chopping blocks), a cleaver and knives.

Historical Notes: Originally, a 'shamble' was a butcher's slaughterhouse or scene of carnage. Thus, 'shamble' was the ideal name for an early meat stall. In 1851, stock (usually cattle) were slaughtered behind a butcher's premises. By 1852-3, the diggings were too crowded for slaughter yards. Pastoralists from nearby runs (like Buninyong) were running more sheep than cattle, and meat sold on the diggings tended to be mutton. This mutton was usually scrawny, but very cheap compared to other foods and was often eaten for breakfast, lunch and dinner. *The Invalid Digger,* by S. T. Gill, shows how diggers stored their meat by hanging it from the ridge of their tent, in the open air.

MINERS' CHAPEL

The idea that the Sabbath Day should be set apart for worship and rest was strongly held during the 1850s. On the goldfields, no work was done on Sundays, and many diggers attended a church service of some kind. Our building represents the first rough shelters which acted as churches for all denominations on the goldfields.

Such buildings were made of canvas, wooden slabs and bark and were hastily thrown up. Inside can be seen a pulpit made of rough-cut timber, a table for the minister's use and a plain wooden cross. Worshippers sat on wooden benches placed in rows on the earth floor, which was thick with dust through summer, wet and muddy through winter. These buildings were among the first schools on Ballarat, until special buildings were erected for that purpose.

WHIPS AND WHIMS

As mine shafts became deeper, man-powered windlasses were replaced by more powerful horse-operated machines. The simplest of these was the horse-whip. The kibble in the shaft was attached to one end of a rope passing through two pulleys suspended above the shaft. The other end was harnessed to a horse. When the horse walked forwards, the kibble was raised. As the horse retraced its steps, the kibble was lowered.

Whims were used in shafts extending up to 570 feet in depth. These machines operated kibbles in twin shafts. As the horse walked around a central drum, the kibble in one shaft was raised and that in the other was lowered. The harness was made so that, when the horse walked in the reverse direction, the raising and lowering of the kibbles was also reversed.

PUDDLING MACHINE

As diggers banded together, and more powerful horse-operated machinery was installed, miners had greater quantities of material to wash. Puddling machines were developed to break up and separate stiff clays from gravel. Cartloads of gravel were tipped into a circular trough lined with timber lathes. Water was run into the trough, and two harrows were dragged through the gravel by a horse walking around its edge. This process separated clay from washdirt and reduced the amount of final panning and cradling needed to recover the gold.

CALIFORNIAN PUMP

It was not always possible to site puddling machines right on a creek-side, and water supply was a serious problem. The Californian pump was one of many ingenious ways in which water was raised or channelled. This machine is essentially a wooden channel, with one end in the water supply and the other in the puddling machine trough. Water is lifted up through it by wooden blades mounted on a rubber belt. The belt was turned by a man operating a windlass.

FLUME

Where water was in short supply, it was sometimes carried from distant creeks or dams in an open race or channel, cut in the ground along a contour. Sometimes, when water had to be carried across a valley, a wooden "flume" or trough was built. Our flume powers a waterwheel.

LEMONADE TENT

In the early days, lemonade and coffee tents were common on the diggings. Until 1854, the diggings were officially "dry". That is to say, the sale of alcohol was banned, in an effort to help officials maintain law and order. Lemonade and coffee tents were the only places where thirsty diggers could buy a drink: coffee, lemonade, ginger beer, soda water and cordials. Often, at the back of the tent, "sly grog" was also dispensed. It was usually rum, and very expensive.

RED HILL MINE

The original Red Hill Mine was a deep lead alluvial mine on Bakery Hill, on the Ballarat East goldfields. An 1858 lithograph, celebrating the discovery of the famous Welcome Nugget, was the reference for this mine.

Our Mine: Our interpretation of the Red Hill Mine focuses on deep lead mining from 1857-8 and illustrates the developmental link between the early, surface alluvial mining of our Diggings and the quartz mining which continued into the 20th century.

The surface display shows the buildings and plant typical of a deep lead alluvial mine, including a poppet head, engine house, boiler, steam engine, winder, beam pump and puddler. As visitors enter the Mine and follow the underground drive, they will find displays illustrating how men worked and the equipment they used in the slimy mud of the deep leads. (Deep lead miners were known as "mudlarks".) One special display re-creates the excitement of finding the Welcome Nugget.

WATERLOO STORE

In 1853, the Waterloo Store, run by R. B. Caul, was located on the flat opposite Golden Point. Our store represents such an early diggings business, supplying all types of goods, from food to small pieces of mining equipment. It is made of split slab walls on a round pole framework, with a tarpaulin roof – a common type of building before, and during, the gold rushes.

CHINESE VILLAGE

The Chinese Village at Sovereign Hill is based on an early photograph of the Golden Point Chinese Village. Chinese were unwelcome in goldrush Victoria and relations between Chinese and European diggers became so tense that the Government set up Chinese Protectorates. These corresponded to the official mining areas and were placed under the jurisdiction of a Chinese Protector.

Our Chinese Village: Our village shows that most Chinese dwellings were canvas tents, set out in rows and numbered. Within Protectorate villages, there were usually six or eight men to a tent. The villages were all-male communities, most intending to win gold and return to China.

Tents which are open to view show differences which illustrate the variety amongst village residents. One tent would have been occupied by newcomers, judging by its contents, which are almost entirely of Chinese origin. Another, with European contents, shows how many Chinese soon adopted European dress, bedding and other household items. A third has few contents of any kind. Its owners may have been more interested in opium and gambling than in seeking gold.

From the pig pens, chicken coops and garden beds, visitors learn that the Chinese kept poultry and animals, and grew vegetables. Cooking and eating were often done communally, with a common fireplace located outside the tents.

An early photograph of the village at Golden Point also shows many rough wooden buildings, some of which were selected for our Village.

TEMPLE

A good description of the Golden Point temple (or "joss house") was found in a January 1860 edition of the *Ballarat Star*. This, together with the temple building seen in an early photograph of the Golden Point village, was the basic reference for the Sovereign Hill building. A further reference was a 1950s photograph of the Main Road temple. This temple was known to have been removed to Main Road from Golden Point earlier this century, and there is strong evidence that it was the same building referred to by the *Star* and seen in the early photograph.

The interior is set up as a typical temple dedicated to the warrior god, Quan Gong, who was associated in Chinese minds with peace, stability and prosperity. As such, he was a popular god with the Chinese on many Australian goldfields. A figurine of the god is on the altar, his horse is represented on a small table beside the altar and his sword stands nearby.

At the front, to the left, is an altar to Choi Bak, god of wealth. Note also the brick prayer burner, the pigeon holes to hold fortune papers, and the small altar to Mun Goon, the door god. As noted by the *Ballarat Star*, a small area was partitioned off for the temple keeper, and this is represented here.

SCRIBE'S HUT

Each Chinese area had a scribe. He translated regulations and other official documents, he kept accounts for the diggers, wrote letters home and read replies for those who were illiterate. Our Scribe's Hut shows his tools of trade – papers, ink block, brushes and brush-stands.

HERBALIST'S HUT

Poor living conditions on the goldfields meant disease and malnutrition. The herbalist was needed to provide herbs and potions to treat health problems. Behind the counter in his hut is an array of drawers to store ingredients. His scales hang from the wall and a large herb chopper sits on the floor.

STORE

Each village elected a headman who liaised with the Chinese Protector and ensured that all rules and regulations were followed. The headman usually ran the store, which carried daily provisions such as rice, sugar, tea, oil and domestic utensils.

Historical Notes: Ballarat's Chinese were mostly from the region of Canton. To discourage all Chinese from coming to the goldfields, the Government levied an expensive tax of £10 (pounds) per head on those landing at Victorian ports. So, the Chinese landed in South Australia and walked to Ballarat and Bendigo. Although the Chinese were good miners, the amount of gold they sent back to China is not really known.

CHINESE PROTECTOR'S OFFICE

The Chinese Protector's Office is located on the other side of the Township, near the Wheelwright's. A grainy photograph, plans dating from 1857 and descriptions in the Protector's official letters were used as references for the facade and internal layout of this building.

Our Building: The interior of this building is not set out as a re-created 1850s interior. Rather, it contains a modern display where visitors can learn more about the functions of the Protector and the Government Camp in general, through displays of pictures, plans and documents. The administration of the goldfields, the problems of establishing order in such turbulent times, and the background to the story of the Chinese on the goldfields are complex topics, much in need of explanation.

Historical Notes: The original office was occupied by the Chinese Protector, an official whose job it was to supervise the Chinese diggers on the goldfields. He located sites for their camps and set out the positions for their tents; he settled disputes between Chinese and European miners over mining matters; he represented the Chinese in court cases; and he kept a watchful eye on the numbers in the Chinese area.

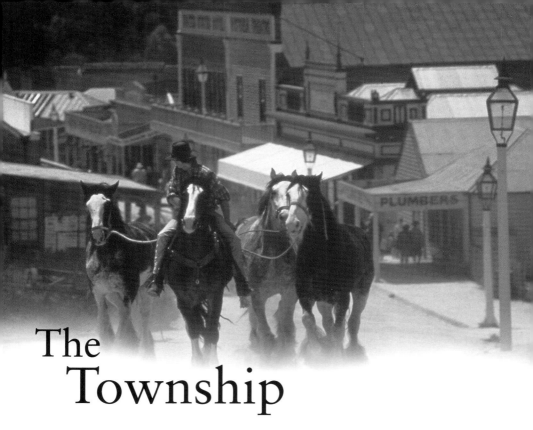

The Township

By December 1851 (four months after the discovery of gold in the area), W. S. Urquhart had completed a survey which sited a township west of the diggings. In May 1852, Ballarat township was proclaimed and, in June, the first land sales were held. Businessmen flocked to Ballarat, confident that an ever-increasing population would mean strong demands for goods and services. Main Street, Sovereign Hill, represents this development of a more stable community on Ballarat's goldfields.

DILGES' BLACKSMITH'S SHOP

This building is based on a photograph of Dilges' forge in Sebastopol.

Our Building: Sovereign Hill's blacksmith shows the varied business of an 1850s smithy, as visitors watch the blacksmith make simple mining and domestic ironware, using huge bellows to keep the furnace coals glowing. An important part of the blacksmith's work is the shoeing of Sovereign Hill's working horses.

Historical Notes: A skilled blacksmith was essential in mid-19th century towns. In the age of the horse, much of the smithy's trade was shoeing horses. The smith was also needed to forge machinery for goldmining. He sharpened mine tools and made handles for windlasses, "spiders" to hold candles in mine walls and other equipment.

As alluvial mining gave way to deeper, company quartz mining, more powerful machinery was needed. The humble smithy was replaced by the great foundries of Ballarat, such as the Phoenix Foundry in Armstrong Street. Yet, most mines still needed their own forge for shoeing mine horses and repairing mining tools and small machines.

CARVER & DALTON AUCTION AND SALE ROOMS

The original Carver & Dalton Auction Rooms stood near the George Hotel, in Lydiard Street. An 1855 drawing of the original was used as a reference for our representation, together with 1857 newspaper notices (giving building dimensions) for the sale of the Auction Rooms.

Our Building: The Sovereign Hill building is closed to visitors because it houses our Education Office. A small representation of John Carver's office can be viewed from outside. Its high desk, stool and bookcase are typical of the period.

Historical Notes: John Carver and William Dalton conducted an auctioneering business in Geelong and Ballarat. Carver ran the Ballarat branch, until it folded in 1857. He was the official agent to the Ballarat Court of Mines and was a member of the first Ballarat West Municipal Council in 1856.

HOPE BAKERY

An 1850s photograph of the original Hope Bakery in Seymour Street, Soldiers' Hill, was the reference for our building. The bread cart standing outside tells us the business was run by George Lovitt and George Briant.

Our Building: The Hope Bakery produces delicious bread, biscuits and pies using a wood-fired brick oven. Recipes of the 1850s are followed as closely as possible. These called for white flour, as the Victorians were proud of their refining processes and did not favour wholemeal bread.

Historical Notes: Mid-19th century bakeries had two functions: supplying Ballarat with its "daily bread" and servicing more extravagant needs. Advertisements of the day tell us that the Hope Bakery catered for "Pic Nics, Balls and Suppers" and supplied "Biscuits, Pies, Tarts, Small Cakes" and "Cakes for Special Occasions".

RED HILL PHOTOGRAPHIC ROOMS

The photographic rooms at Red Hill, on Main Road, Ballarat, were run by William Ellis around 1854. He was joined by A.V. Smith, who then took over the business in 1857.

Our Building: Today, visitors enjoy dressing in period costume for Victorian-style portraits, taken with a camera modelled on the sliding box camera used at the time.

Historical Notes: The 1850s Red Hill Photographic Rooms originally specialised in daguerreotypes, the first commercially successful photographs. They are one-off photographs taken on a silvered copper plate. Finely detailed and fragile, they sold, cased, for about 30 shillings.

By 1856, this method was being replaced by the cheaper and more versatile wet-plate method. A glass plate was covered with collodion (a highly-explosive solution of cotton wool in nitric acid) and sensitised in silver nitrate solution. A portrait was taken while the plate was still wet, the result being a glass negative. This was used to produce ambrotypes (imitation daguerreotypes) or prints on paper.

ALEX KELLY, AUCTIONEER

An 1861 lithograph by Hermann Deutsch, a German engraver, was used as a reference for this building.

Our Building: Alex Kelly's office contains furniture and equipment typical of the period – a high desk and stool, a pigeon-hole cupboard, a safe and a horse measure.

Historical Notes: Alex Kelly lived in Ballarat for nearly thirty years as a stock and station agent. He was an official of the local Presbyterian Church and a respected citizen.

Diggers moving around early goldfields had no wish to carry many belongings. They bought what they needed on arrival and employed auctioneers, who operated from tents, to sell their possessions before moving on. As Ballarat became a township, auctioneers expanded their business activities into land and property, and the selling of livestock and farm produce.

BATH'S HOTEL STABLES

The facade of this building was taken from an H. Deutsch lithograph of 1861, which shows the arrival of the great Leviathan Coach from Geelong.

Our Building: Bath's Hotel Stables help us to recapture some of the excitement of the age of the horse, and of horse transport. Sovereign Hill's working horses are used to wind the whim, drag the rakes of the puddling machine and pull the coaches, drays and carriages. Some of these horses are stabled here for short periods during the day.

Historical Notes: In 1853, Thomas Bath built the first hotel in Ballarat, on the site in Lydiard Street now occupied by Craig's Hotel. This was a roughly-erected building, and after six months, it was replaced by a fine hotel of two storeys. On a block of land between the hotel and Sturt Street, Bath built the stables shown in Deutsch's lithograph. Offices at the front of the premises were occupied by Alex Kelly and the Australian Stage Company (then proprietors of the Cobb & Co. coaching service).

AUSTRALIAN STAGE COMPANY

The H. Deutsch lithograph of 1861 shows the Australian Stage Company's office in Lydiard Street South. This company was formed in 1861, by the amalgamation of several coach lines, many of which operated under the name of Cobb & Co. It retained the title of Cobb & Co. which carried much goodwill.

Our Building: Our office shows visitors a Dickensian high desk and stool, a twine container and travellers' trunks. Belongings are pigeon-holed according to their destination.

Historical Notes: Freeman Cobb was a young American. With three other Americans, he started a carrying service in Melbourne, in 1853 and, later that year, developed the Cobb & Co. Telegraph Line, a coach service between Melbourne and Victoria's goldfields.

Cobb & Co. became popular because of its fast, safe and reliable service. Freeman Cobb also imported the famed Concord coaches from America. Their leather thoroughbracing and light construction made them unusually comfortable. The Cobb & Co. line came to Ballarat only after May 1856, when Freeman Cobb sold his company to Thomas Davis, an American operating a Ballarat coach service. Davis kept the title of Cobb & Co.

BALLARAT TIMES OFFICE

An 1859 lithograph by the French artist, François Cogné, was the reference for this building.

Our Building: The *Ballarat Times* Office contains 19th century printing presses, the oldest of which was built by Hopkinson & Cope, of England, in 1857. The improved Albion Press dates from the 1860s. Other presses come from London and Cleveland, Ohio.

Historical Notes: The founding editor was the fiery Henry Seekamp who was gaoled for sedition when he supported rebellious diggers at the time of the Eureka Rebellion, in 1854.

C. SPENCER, CONFECTIONER

This shop is part of the *Ballarat Times* building, the facade of which was taken from the François Cogné lithograph of 1859.

Our Building: Today, the confectionery sold at C. Spencer's shop is made in Brown's Confectionery Manufactory, at Sovereign Hill. The glistening boiled sweets are displayed temptingly in large, glass jars.

Historical Notes: It seems that Charles Spencer, in fact, owned the block and operated a business there for several years. He was a baker, grocer and confectioner, and probably made a great variety of sweets on the premises.

CLARKE BROTHERS, GROCERS

The 1859 Cogné lithograph of the junction of Main Road and Victoria Street provided the reference for the facade of this building.

Our Building: Clarke Bros. Grocery is rich with the atmosphere of early Ballarat stores. Here, visitors can smell the aromas of soaps, spices, herbs and coffee; they can buy baskets and wooden spoons, biscuits and liquorice sticks. At the back of the shop is a magnificent coffee-grinding machine, for the Clarke brothers were well-known coffee merchants.

Historical Notes: Thomas and Richard Clarke came to Melbourne from England in 1850 and moved to Ballarat after the Gold Rush had started. They eventually established a grocery business, and it is believed that the Victoria Street shop represented here was, in fact, their first. It was opened early in 1857, and apparently, two more shops were opened by the Clarke brothers in the following two years. Such general stores carried a wide range of goods from cheeses, pickles and teas, to buckets, picks and other simple mining equipment.

The Clarke brothers' partnership lasted until 1864, when Richard moved to Geelong and established his own grocery business. Thomas continued the grocery business in Ballarat into the 1890s.

T. MURPHY, TENTMAKER

A Cogné lithograph of Main Road, in 1859, was the reference for this shop. It shows a tentmaker sitting in the doorway, hand-sewing a length of canvas.

Historical Notes: Obviously, the tentmaker was a busy man in a goldfields town, where many diggers had no permanent homes and lived under canvas. In the days before named streets and roads, he also made the colourful flags used by diggers, tradesmen and storekeepers to proclaim their whereabouts amid the sea of canvas that was early Ballarat.

REES & BENJAMIN, WATCH & CLOCKMAKERS

As shown in the 1859 Cogné lithograph, this odd-shaped little shop stood beside Murphy's, at the south-west corner of Main Road and Barkly Street.

Our Building: In the Sovereign Hill building today, a silversmith fashions a wide variety of items based on the favourite styles of the period.

Historical Notes: The original firm of Rees & Benjamin sold watches and jewellery, together with instruments for land and mining surveys. Their main sales, however, came from clocks. In the 1850s, these were remarkably cheap, being mass-produced in America and exported by the hundreds of thousands to Great Britain and thence to the Colonies.

Rees & Benjamin also sold "Colonial" jewellery, with which the successful diggers bedecked their ladies to show off their new-found wealth. This was probably fairly cheap jewellery, of popular design, imported from Britain and Europe.

POST OFFICE

The Ballarat Post Office building represented at Sovereign Hill originally stood on the south-west corner of Mair Street and Lydiard Street. The original plans, drawn in 1854 by the then Clerk of Works to the Colonial Architect, together with a drawing by goldfields artist, S.T. Gill, were used as references for the re-creation of this building at Sovereign Hill.

Our Building: This attractive weatherboard building, with a shingle roof, is certain to please admirers of colonial architecture. It incorporates the Postmaster's office and residence. The office here is of interest with its high desk, wooden stamps, sealing wax, pigeon holes and bags of mail awaiting dispatch.

This is a fully-functioning post office, which provides EFTPOS, postal and philatelic services. Mail posted from here, and from the old-style red pillar box outside the Entrance Building, will bear Sovereign Hill's own postmark.

The residence, which can be viewed at the back of the building, is furnished with fine examples of Victorian furniture, in particular, the chairs and chaise-longue in the living room, which have been beautifully restored. On the other side of the building, you may meet some of our volunteers cooking in the Post Office kitchen.

Historical Notes: In 1854, a twice-weekly mail service operated out of Ballarat to Geelong and Melbourne. Mail came regularly from England and took about three months to reach Ballarat. In 1858, the building represented at Sovereign Hill was replaced by a bluestone post office on the corner of Lydiard Street and Sturt Street which, in turn, was replaced by the present Ballarat Post Office, in 1864.

The attractive Victorian cottage garden shows many examples of typical flowers, herbs and vegetables which were popular in the goldrush era. The Postmaster who lived in the original building was Charles Pain, who was Postmaster in Ballarat from 1853 to 1859.

N.B. Viewing area at rear of building.

BRIGHT VIEW COTTAGE

The original section of this cottage was built in 1858. It stood at
Greendale, near Ballan, 30 kilometres east of Ballarat. Bright View was
donated to Sovereign Hill by Mr D. Fraser and was the first building on
our site.

Our Building: Today, Bright View houses the offices of the Executive
Director and administrative staff.

Historical Notes: This charming weatherboard cottage was originally the
home of the D'Arcy family (farmers around Greendale for over 100
years), until its purchase by Mr Fraser. The architecture is typical of the
Colonial period, with its double-gabled roof, twelve-paned windows and
return verandah. The building is separated from its extensions to the
west by a covered skillion.

The garden has a typically geometric Victorian design. Plantings were
selected using the earliest nurserymen's catalogues in Ballarat. In the
garden, you will find a bunya bunya pine (Araucaria bidwillii), a garrya
eliptica and a tulip tree (Liriodendron tulipifera), whilst two eucalypts
(E. viminalis) are adjacent to the verandah. The latter were indigenous to
Ballarat. The privet hedges, the devonensia rose which arches across the
gateway, and a herb garden, outline the garden's basic structure.

N.B. Only the garden is open for public inspection.

WILLIAM PROCTOR, COACHBUILDER

An 1861 photograph and detailed newspaper descriptions tell us that the
original manufactory stood in Sturt Street.

Our Building: On display here are some of Sovereign Hill's significant
collection of historical vehicles.

Historical Notes: William Proctor established his Ballarat business in late
1860. At the rear of the premises was a smith's shop with six furnaces.
Proctor built a variety of horse-drawn vehicles using English and
American Ash and Hickory.

R. & C. TUNBRIDGE, TIMBER MERCHANTS

An 1861 photograph of the north-east corner of Doveton and Sturt Streets was used as a reference for this business. The sheds and offices stood in the timber yard on the corner, immediately beside Proctor's Manufactory.

Historical Notes: The business was founded in 1854 and, soon, a thriving wholesale trade handling clothing, furniture and household goods was also developed by the family.

WHEELWRIGHT'S PLANT

Most of the machines in our Wheelwright's Plant were manufactured by the Defiance Machine Works, U.S.A. The Defiance Works was one of the most prestigious companies supplying specialised wheelwrighting machinery in the second half of the 19th century.

Our Building: The Wheelwright's stands beside William Proctor's Coach Manufactory. Our plant consists of four main sections: component manufacture, timber drying, assembly and timber bending. In the days of horse-drawn vehicles, wheelwrighting was an extremely important trade. Our Wheelwright's Plant offers visitors the rare opportunity to see demonstrations of this fascinating trade, as it was carried out in the 1890s, in its heyday.

Sovereign Hill's coachbuilders and wheelwrights build and repair all of our extensive range of horse-drawn vehicles. Outside commissions from all over Australia, and export work, are also accepted.

Historical Notes: In an 1860s coachbuilding factory, the successful completion of a vehicle required the individual application of several men's specialised skills. Visitors will quickly see the contrast between the Wheelwright's Plant and the earlier coachbuilding and wheelwrighting processes next door. The Wheelwright's Plant, circa 1890, shows wheelwrighting technology at its height, using flat belt-and-pulley driven machinery. This unique collection of machinery has been restored and set up under the supervision of the former owner, who has also trained staff who operate the plant.

GOVERNMENT CAMP – SOVEREIGN HILL LODGE

In the 1850s, every goldfields township, including Ballarat, needed
a form of colonial administration centre. At Sovereign Hill, we have
re-created part of Ballarat's Government Camp as it was in 1857.

Our Buildings: Our representation of Government Camp provides us
with a modern accommodation complex known as Sovereign Hill Lodge.
Bookings may be made at the Lodge or at the Bookings Desk in the
Sovereign Hill Entrance Building.

Historical Notes: The first Government Camp was set up by the resident
Gold Commissioner at Golden Point, in 1851. As Ballarat's diggings
grew, the Government Camp was moved to the high ground bordered by
Sturt Street, Mair Street and what later became known as Camp Street.

SPEEDWELL STREET

As early goldrush Ballarat settled down in the mid-1850s, and diggers
drifted into paid employment in mines or local industries, they began
to make a family and a community life in Ballarat. Tents on the diggings
gave way to a more substantial township of timber and brick. In
Speedwell Street, visitors catch a glimpse of everyday lives in this new,
civilised Ballarat.

Our Buildings: Speedwell Street's houses have been created by working
from a variety of period photographs. Each represents a common type
of dwelling found in Ballarat in the late 1850s.

This was a time with as many inconveniences as there were elegances.
In Speedwell Street, you can step back into family life as it actually was
in the 1850s, with charming furniture and no running water, cosy wood
fires and draughty outdoor "dunnies". You may meet some of our
volunteers who "live" in these homes, helping to show how different
families lived in Ballarat. We have woven the following stories about
them.

DAVIDSONS' COTTAGE

Mr Davidson, a mining engineer, is quite well-off and has added an extra gable to his house to provide rooms for his large family. The kitchen and the laundry at the rear of the house are well fitted out. This engineer has two hobbies: investing in mining companies and collecting minerals – and his wife dearly wishes that he would give up the first. She is a good mother, but has never really liked living in Australia and is constantly worried by her husband's speculations. Her garden features many herbs, grown for medicinal purposes, for Mrs Davidson does not keep good health.

CHAMBERS' COTTAGE

Mr Chambers, his wife and their young family live in a new single-gable cottage. He is a shop assistant in one of the more prestigious shops on Main Street, but is determined to improve his place in society. So, while his wife looks after their young children, he studies at home or attends improving lectures at the Mechanics' Institute, trying to better himself.

TAYLORS' COTTAGE

The District Surveyor, Mr Taylor, is often away from home and his house is not open to visitors.

WAIN'S COTTAGE

The Widow Wain lives alone in her small timber cottage. Having lost her husband in a mining accident, she now ekes out her living by mending and cleaning ladies' bonnets.

ST. IVES

St. Ives is the home of a successful barrister. This imposing brick building, with its slate roof and timber verandah, is not open to visitors, as the owners have returned to the "old country" for an extended holiday. In fact, St. Ives provides space for curatorial staff offices and a reference library.

RED HILL NATIONAL SCHOOL

This neat building is made of grey-painted weatherboard with a shingle roof. Its creation was a joint project between the Victorian Education Department and the then Ballarat Historical Park Association.

Our Building: The schoolhouse is a fully-activated exhibit in which visiting students experience 1850s school life. They dress in period costume, sit at simple desks and learn arithmetic, spelling, grammar, reading and drawing.

Historical Notes: The Red Hill National School began in a tent as the Warrenheip Gully School. On the diggings, canvas was very expensive, and in September 1854, the Master reported that "some ruffians had attempted to carry off the school tent", probably to use on their claims. The tent was replaced by a simple wooden building with a shingle roof, situated on Main Road in the midst of mining activity. Goldfields schoolmasters faced many problems, and attendances were unpredictable as families moved from one diggings to another. The National Schools' system was based on the Irish education system, and these schools were the forerunners of the government schools of today.

The 1850s was a time when most people placed a strong emphasis on the value of education, realising the advantages that the ability to read and write would give them. Groups of local townsmen, therefore, soon banded together on the goldfields to provide education for the children of the diggers and tradesmen. They formed committees of Local Patrons which saw that the regulations of the Board of National Education in Melbourne were observed.

N.B. Visitors are welcome to watch children at their lessons.

ST. PETER'S CHURCH OF ENGLAND SCHOOL

In Victoria, in the 1850s, education was controlled by two separate bodies: the National School Board and the Denominational School Board. St. Peter's represents an 1850s Denominational School.

Our Building: Here, students experience a two-day live-in programme in which they wear historical costume and follow the 1850s curriculum. Visitors enjoy watching 19th century-style lessons presented by costumed teachers from the Victorian Department of Education.

Historical Notes: The "official" denomination of Australia, in the early goldrush days, was the Church of England. This was the religion of the Mother Country, England, and favoured by the majority of Colonial residents.

Erected on Yuille Swamp Reserve and sited near the corner of Mair and Pleasant Streets, in Ballarat, the school was built in 1861 for £200 (pounds). Though a humble weatherboard construction, it was designed by H. R. Caselli, who was later designed the Ballarat Town Hall, the Ballarat City Fire Brigade, and several Ballarat and district churches. While the building was erected as a schoolhouse, it was also used as a church. In 1864, the Denominational and National School Boards were abolished and St. Peter's School became the Pleasant Street Common School No. 695.

N.B. Visitors are welcome to watch children at their lessons.

LINTON COTTAGE

A photograph of a house in Linton, a town 30 kilometres south-west of Ballarat, provided the reference for "Linton Cottage".

Our Building: This weatherboard building illustrates the more elaborate cottage-style which developed as Ballarat grew. Behind the cottage is a typical goldrush vegetable garden (complete with scarecrow). "Linton Cottage" is not open to visitors because it provides staff facilities.

N.B. Visitors are welcome to view the rear garden.

ROBINSON & WAYNE'S APOTHECARIES' HALL

Cogné's 1859 drawing of Main Road was the reference for this building.

Our Building: On the roof is a mortar and pestle (symbol of the apothecary). An excellent collection of apothecaries' tools and utensils is on display, and the consulting room "belongs" to Dr. Wakefield, who came to Ballarat in the mid-1850s. It contains a patient's couch and various pieces of medical equipment.

Historical Notes: The "apothecary" was the 1850s equivalent of today's pharmacist, and his certificate also licensed him to practise medicine and dentistry.

COLONIAL BANK OF AUSTRALASIA

This building was referenced from a photograph of Lydiard Street, published by Solomon and Bardwell, in 1861. The fine counter and fittings came from the State Savings Bank of Victoria in Creswick.

Historical Notes: It seems that the Bank of New South Wales, the first bank in Ballarat, opened in a tent, in 1853. Permanent buildings and other banking companies quickly followed as Ballarat grew. In function, goldrush banks were similar to banks today. There were no governmental regulations, however, and a life's savings are safer in a bank today than they were then.

GOLD OFFICE

This building is based on an 1861 photograph of Lydiard Street by Solomon and Bardwell.

Historical Notes: The gold office was important during the Gold Rush. Miners brought their gold here to be weighed and purchased and, from 1853, were given as much as £4 (pounds) an ounce. Purchased gold was stored in a heavy safe until the gold escort carried it to Melbourne. From 1855, some Australian gold was used at the Sydney Mint, but most was exported to Europe, to be turned into coin or jewellery.

UNIVERSAL TRANSIT OFFICE

A simple line drawing by J. Butler (c.1856) provided the reference for Sovereign Hill's representation of the original Universal Transit Office, which stood in Main Road.

Our Building: The Universal Transit Office introduces the fact that there were several coaching lines to the goldfields and that there was fierce competition between them.

Historical Notes: The Estafette Line of Coaches was operated by Baldwin Davis Clarke, an American entrepreneur. He appointed agents in the various townships to oversee booking operations and George Binstead, of the Universal Transit Office, was one such agent.

Coaches ran daily between Ballarat and Geelong, and Ballarat and Melbourne. It was a proud boast of the company that anyone leaving by the 6 a.m. coach would reach Geelong in time for the 1.00 p.m. steamer to Melbourne.

By the end of the 1850s, the Estafette Line was bought by another American, Thomas Davies, who took control of several coaching lines and ran them under the name of Cobb & Co.

NEW YORK BAKERY

An early photograph of the original bakery, which stood in Lydiard Street, was used as a reference for this building.

Our Building: Much of the interior design of our bakery was based on advice from Alfred Reid, a son of the founder, John Reid. The New York Bakery is fully licensed and serves meals and light refreshments.

Historical Notes: The portraits overlooking the dining area are of John Reid and his wife. John Reid, a son of a German nobleman, learnt the trade of baker in New York.

UNITED STATES HOTEL

François Cogné's drawing of Main Road shows the United States Hotel beside the Victoria Theatre.

Our Building: The impressive bar fittings came from an 1850s pub, near Bendigo. Labels on the 1850s black bottles on the shelf were reproduced from originals. The elegant dining room has a typically rich Victorian decor and a graceful lithograph of Queen Victoria and her family. The Theatre Retiring Room, above the bar, is closed to visitors because it is used for conferences and private functions.

Historical Notes: The original United States Hotel was a noisy, boisterous place where diggers met at the end of the day to chat, play bagatelle or billiards, or attend meetings. It also offered accommodation for about eighty.

The United States Hotel was started by three Americans – Henry Moody, Rufus Smith and Albion Nichols. A theatre (the Adelphi) was built as part of the hotel complex, but both were burnt down in December 1855, in a fire which killed Albion Nichols. A new hotel/theatre complex was rapidly erected by Moody and Smith; the hotel opened by New Year 1856, and the theatre (the Victoria) opened on 16 February, 1856.

VICTORIA THEATRE

A François Cogné print of 1859 shows this theatre standing next to the United States Hotel, in Main Road, Ballarat.

Our Building: The Victoria Theatre, though wooden and cheaply built, was opulently decorated. Our theatre reflects this Victorian taste, with its 'marble' columns, exuberantly decorated balcony, proscenium arch and crystal chandelier.

Historical Notes: The original Victoria Theatre held some 2,500 people. Of the many famous performers who starred at the Victoria Theatre, none was more famous (or infamous) than the Irish actress, Lola Montez, whose erotic Spider Dance provoked much public discussion.

CRITERION STORE

An original 1859 François Cogné lithograph was the reference for the exterior of the Criterion Store.

Our Building: The twelve-foot plate glass windows, re-created in our store, were a notable feature of the original. The Criterion Store sells a wide range of clothing and accessories. The interior boasts large mirrors, extensive and ornate ceiling roses, and cedar display cabinets. Delicate original lithographs of the latest French fashions are displayed to inform the ladies of the Colony of the newest fashions.

Historical Notes: Mr David Jones, a Welshman, established his "Criterion House" in 1853, in Ballarat. Soon after, he went into partnership with a Mr Hemmingway, calling the premises the "Criterion Store".

CHARLIE NAPIER HOTEL

The facade of this hotel was based on an 1856 drawing by J.E. Butler.

Our Building: The "Charlie" was designed to appeal to Ballarat's middle class men. Its bar was a focal point of social life on Main Road. Our Ladies' and Gentlemen's Parlours provide quiet retreats. Both contain writing equipment – an essential feature of goldfields hotels. There is also a large dining room and a bagatelle room. Upstairs, the bedrooms show that only married couples had a private room – men paid for a bed only, in a shared room. The Meeting Room, opposite, is permanently set for a Masonic Meeting. (There is some evidence that John Gibbs, the owner, had connections with the Masons.) The room contains impressive mid-Victorian furniture donated by the Talbot Masonic Lodge.

Historical Notes: The original Charlie Napier Hotel, on Main Road, was reminiscent of an old English coaching inn. Established in 1854 by Robert Underwood and John Gibbs, it was named after the popular British Military General, to encourage patrons.

MECHANICS' INSTITUTE & FREE LIBRARY

This original 1860s building, from Scarsdale, near Ballarat, was moved to Sovereign Hill in 1972.

Our Building: During winter, a cheery fire invites visitors to stop and chat with our costumed volunteers who bring this building to life. Books on display date from the 1850s and the librarian's desk is from the Shire of Talbot & Clunes.

Historical Notes: Mechanics' Institutes were the forerunners of adult education. In the 1850s, the word "mechanic" referred to men who earned their living by manual labour. Many diggers saw education and expanded knowledge as the key to advancement in life.

SOUTHSEA OIL COMPANY

A Cogné lithograph of Main Road, in 1859, shows this small business situated beside the Edinburgh Boot & Shoe Mart.

Historical Notes: Until the mid-nineteenth century, whale oil fuelled many domestic lamps. Paraffin, naphtha and lubricating oils for machinery were being distilled from coal, for commercial purposes, by 1850s and by the 1860s, paraffin oil (kerosene) was widely used in lamps.

EDINBURGH BOOT & SHOE MART

A Cogné lithograph of Main Road in 1859 was the reference for the facade of this building. The rear of the building is used for storage.

Our Building: The Edinburgh Boot & Shoe Mart's window display features footwear and related items available in goldrush Ballarat.

Historical Notes: Wellingtons and Napoleons (the tall, men's boots) owe their names to the famous military leaders. Ladies' ankle boots which covered the ankle (preserving modesty) were popular with crinoline skirts.

CLARKE BROTHERS, TINSMITHS

This building originally stood in Humffray Street North and was bequeathed to Sovereign Hill by "Tinker" Clarke on his death, in 1971. His father had been a tinker on Ballarat's goldfields, and the business had been in the family since then.

Our Building: This iron-roofed wooden building consists of three rooms: the workshop, the main shop and an office. In the workshop, visitors see the tinsmith cutting tin plate and sheet copper to make pie plates, scone and biscuit cutters, candle lamps and similar wares.

Historical Notes: In the 1850s, tinsmiths made such goods, but they also made and repaired zinc-roofing and guttering, made lanterns and handled some imported goods such as stoves and electroplated and enamelled ware.

JOHN ALLOO'S RESTAURANT

An 1850s sketch by goldfields artist, S.T. Gill, was used as a basis for this building. The original restaurant stood in Main Road and was popular with Chinese and European diggers alike.

Our Building: This simple eating house has a plain interior with wooden candle holders and salt and sugar boxes on the tables.

Historical Notes: We have no record of the foods served by John Alloo. It seems likely that both Chinese food and the European soups, stews and pies, shown in Gill's sketches, would have been available.

John Alloo's acted as a booking office for the Royal Mail Estafette Line of coaches to Geelong, at least until early 1857. Thomas Davies, who took over Cobb & Co. in 1856, also gained control of the Estafette Line. Therefore, the reference to the Cobb & Co. coaching service in some of the Gill sketches of this restaurant, probably indicates that Alloo's subsequently acted as a booking office for Davies' Lines, since Davies used the term Cobb & Co. for his whole enterprise.

N.B. This building is sometimes closed for use as a classroom.

SOHO FOUNDRY

An 1850s advertisement for the Soho Works inspired the construction of
this building.

Our Building: Here, visitors see metal-spinning and wood-turning by
skilled craftsmen using steam-powered lathes.

Historical Notes: The Soho Works was founded by Robinson, Thomas
& Co. in 1856. They were iron and brass founders, boiler makers,
pattern makers and engineers. Like other early Ballarat foundries, such
as the Phoenix and the Victoria, the chief function of the Soho Works
was probably to repair cast iron implements and engines. Heavy
machinery was introduced to Ballarat by quartz mining companies in the
late 1850s. The manufacture of heavy mining machinery soon followed.

WESLEYAN CHURCH

This church came from Grenville, near Ballarat. Although built in 1892,
its architectural style – Victorian Carpenter Gothic – was popular from
the 1840s to the 1890s.

Our Building: The church originally served three denominations –
Church of England, Methodist and Presbyterian. By 1977, it was used
by the Uniting Church, but was not used for regular worship after 1993.
In April 1996, the church was moved to Sovereign Hill, having been
donated, with its furniture, by the congregation.

Historical Notes: In March, 1853, the first minute book of Ballarat's
Wesleyan Methodist Church records donations and subscriptions
towards the purchase of a tent to be erected on the Ballarat diggings.
The tent was used for public worship by the Wesleyan congregation,
as a Sunday school and a day school.

A Reverend Vipont was appointed as the first minister in mid-1853, but
he was found to be unsatisfactory and was replaced by Reverend
Theophilus Taylor in February, 1854.

N.B. *This building is open for public inspection on weekends.*

FIRE STATION

This Engine House is based on a photograph of the Smythesdale Fire Brigade Station in the mid-1860s. Smythesdale was a busy goldmining town 18 kilometres south-west of Ballarat, with regular coach services.

Our Building: The original Shand Mason pumping engine, the *Yarrowee*, is on loan to Sovereign Hill from the Smythesdale-Scarsdale Fire Brigade. Fire engines in Victorian days were given names. The Ballarat Fire Brigade appropriately named theirs *Aquarius*, after the Zodiac sign for water.

Historical Notes: In an 1850s goldmining town, crowded with tents and wooden buildings with open fire-places, oil lamps and candles, fire was a constant danger. In 1856, a voluntary fire brigade was formed. Horse-drawn hose carriages and water carts raced to a fire when the alarm bell sounded. To fight a fire, firemen used leather buckets, hooks, ladders and tomahawks (as seen in the rear of the building). Water was very precious. Often they had to pull down buildings in the path of a fire to stop its spread.

EMPIRE BOWLING SALOON

The original Empire Bowling Saloon was known as "one of the most agreeable resorts on the Main Road of Ballarat for those who delight in healthy exercise".

Our Building: The game played at Sovereign Hill is ninepin bowling. This was of German origin, and many variations were played in Britain and brought to the goldfields in the 1850s. It is the exceptional length of the laneways which distinguishes this game from today's American tenpin bowling. A set of rules is available if you wish to test your skill. Or, perhaps you might like to try bagatelle, which is a type of billiards.

Historical Notes: Bowling Saloons were often associated with hotels, providing noisy amusement and companionship for miners, whilst being simple and cheap to set up and operate.

W. DAWSON, BUILDERS AND UNDERTAKERS

Our undertaker's re-creates an original business which operated in Sturt Street Ballarat, in 1861. It was run by Mr W. Dawson, a builder turned-undertaker after a Mr Ash left the partnership.

Our Building: W. Dawson's premises is typical of a well-to-do, 1860s Ballarat undertaker's. Along with an array of coffins, visitors will find decorative timber work – undertaking was often a second trade picked up by builders, carpenters and wheelwrights.

In William Dawson's fine office, you will find reproduction examples of funeral clothing and accessories. On his desk are mourning cards, an account book and a box of trade cards. Please take one! In the workshop, a pot of pitch (for sealing coffins) waits by the stove to be heated. The coach store contains three vehicles: a child's and an adult's hearse, and a horse-drawn coffin-carrier. The latter two were donated in 1973 by Barkell's, undertakers in Clunes and, like the child's hearse, are of early to mid-19th century design. The child's hearse and the patent leather harness were replicated by Sovereign Hill craftsmen.

Historical Notes: Poor living conditions and a lack of fresh food and water meant disease was common in early Ballarat. Mortality rates were high, with nearly 40% of children under five dying.

STEINFELD'S FURNITURE WAREHOUSE

The original building was erected in 1860 in the part of Main Road now known as Bridge Street.

Our Building: Our building has two showrooms. It is leased to a firm of skilled craftsmen who make furniture to mid-19th century designs.

Historical Notes: Emmanuel Steinfeld was born in Silesia, Prussia, and opened his first business in Ballarat in 1856. A well-known figure in the township, he was elected to the Ballarat East Municipal Council in 1861 and became Mayor of Ballarat East from 1866 to 1869. He was much involved with the Ballarat Orphanage, the Fire Brigade, libraries and Masonic circles.

WILLIAM HEWETT'S YARROWEE SOAP & CANDLE WORKS

This business is based on a firm owned by William Hewett whose soap and candle works operated in Mair Street, in the early 1860s. John Jungwirth was a fellmonger (a dealer in animal skins) who conducted his business from the same building.

Our Building: Our re-created factory shows visitors how an 1860s steam-operated plant would have looked. Our candlemaker demonstrates two 19th century mass-production candlemaking techniques. For dipped candles, he uses the Nodding Donkey – a replica of a late 18th century hand-operated dipping apparatus. The later machine is an original 19th century continuous wicking candle-moulding machine. In its day, this machine represented significant advances in the mass production technology of moulding candles. Our candle box label was adapted from Hewett's original label.

Historical Notes: The Industrial Revolution created a heavy demand for candles to light factories, workshops, shops and taverns. In Ballarat, with so many mines, candlemaking was an important local industry. The mid-19th century saw the height of candlemaking technology, with candles being mass-produced efficiently in factories, using imported continuous wicking moulding machines like ours.

BROWN'S CONFECTIONERY MANUFACTORY

This wooden building with a shingled roof represents the hastily-constructed "manufactories" erected in 1850s Ballarat.

Our Building: John Brown – a descendant of the original owner – originally trained Sovereign Hill staff to manufacture a dozen varieties of sweets, all made with the traditional ingredients of glucose, sugar, natural oils and essences. Lolly-making is demonstrated daily, and the lollies are sold at Charles Spencer's Sweet Shop and the Gift Shop.

Historical Notes: Brown's Confectionery Manufactory was established in Dunolly, north of Ballarat, in 1857. The business moved to Ballarat in the late 19th century. In 1974, its traditional sweet-making equipment was transferred to Sovereign Hill.

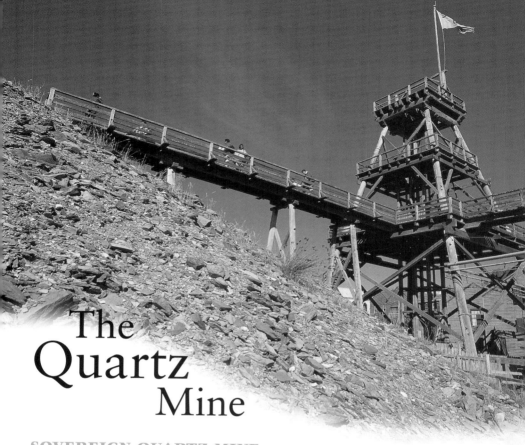

The Quartz Mine

SOVEREIGN QUARTZ MINE

By the early 1860s, as alluvial gold became harder to find, miners began extracting gold from buried quartz reefs. Quartz mining required deeper, more extensive mines, with steam pumping and winding equipment, trolley systems, batteries to crush ore and other equipment to extract gold. Companies were formed to raise capital and most diggers became employees. Faced with increasingly expensive labour and materials, Ballarat's quartz mining ended during World War One.

Sovereign Hill's Quartz Mine illustrates quartz mining on the Ballarat East goldfield from 1860 to 1916, carrying visitors beyond Ballarat's first decade which is depicted in the rest of the Outdoor Museum. The Mine comprises two sections: surface installations and underground displays. It is named after the Sovereign Quartz Mine, which once operated just west of the Township.

POPPET HEAD AND ENGINE HOUSE

The most imposing of the surface installations is the massive timber
Poppet Head. This term is used throughout the Ballarat area, but
elsewhere it may also be known as a Head Frame, Head Gear or Mine
Head. Its function was to support the huge wheels which carried cables
used for raising and lowering cages in the shafts below.

These wheels were operated by the steam-powered winding engine in the
Engine House. Heavy steel winding rope is attached to two engine
drums. As the engine turns, the rope on one drum is paid out while that
on the other drum is wound in. These ropes pass through the roof of the
Engine House, over the wheels at the top of the Poppet Head and down
the shafts to the cages. All men, equipment and mining materials were
carried up and down the shafts in these cages. Our Engine House also
contains a steam-powered compressor which provides compressed air to
drive underground equipment.

BOILER HOUSE

Behind the Engine House is the Boiler House where great wood-fired
furnaces heat two steam-making Cornish Boilers. Stacks of firewood
nearby give some idea of the appetite of these boilers. Stringybark and
Ironbark, cut into metre lengths, is brought to the furnaces on trolleys.
The rails and turntables for these can be seen on the floor of the viewing
area. Steam from the boilers is used to power all the engines of the
Sovereign Quartz Mine and it is even piped up to the Soho Foundry
where it powers the belt-driven machinery in the workshop.

BEAM PUMP

Beam pumps were common on the Ballarat goldfields in the second half of the 19th century. Ballarat East mines were constantly plagued by water leaking into underground workings; pumping out water was a continual task.

In the Engine House, a steam engine turns a large fly wheel and gear wheel. A crank is attached to the gear wheel and to a huge wooden beam which passes through the wall of the Engine House. As the gear wheel turns, the beam moves and its circulating movement is converted to a horizontal movement by a post which pivots at ground level and a second timber beam. In turn, this horizontal movement is converted to a vertical movement by the rocking beam with its counterweight box filled with large rocks. This rocking beam operates a piston plunger pump by means of wooden rods running down into the shaft. Water is raised to the surface through a large diameter pipe called a rising main.

MINE BLACKSMITH

Almost all 19th century mines had a blacksmith's shop to make and repair miners' tools and equipment. It was a very important area for the mine, because the blacksmith also carried out most running repairs. Great speed and ingenuity were required to keep the mine in constant operation, with minimal disruption. Often, the blacksmith assisted the engineer in repairing heavy machinery, although this was also done in the many foundries which were established about Ballarat from the late 1850s.

MINE MANAGER'S COTTAGE

The Mine Manager was the most senior person involved in the day-to-day running of the mine. He was always required to be on hand in case of emergency. So important was his position that his house was usually sited close to the mine and is represented here by a small weatherboard building opposite the Poppet Head.

The Mine Manager's Cottage functions as a Mine Information Centre, housing an interpretive display on 19th century goldmining.

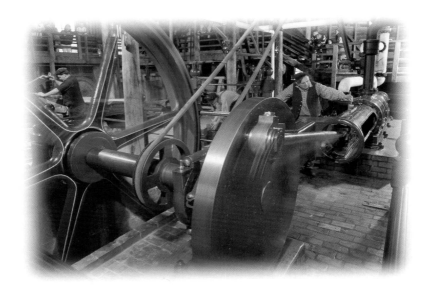

MULLOCK HEAP

The hill beside the Poppet Head is a fine example of a "mullock" or waste rock heap. Formed by tipping excavated mullock from a tramway, this heap is from the original Normanby North Mine. Mullock heaps were common around Ballarat, but most were used as rock-fill for building reservoirs during World War Two.

BATTERY HOUSE

Gold-bearing quartz, excavated from the mine, had to be crushed before the gold was extracted. Crushing was done by stamper batteries like our working ten-head battery. The Battery is driven by a Tandem Compound steam engine, built in 1877 at Ballarat's Phoenix Foundry.

The vertical steam engine, made by G.G. Norman of Ballarat, drives other machines used to extract gold. Also in this building are a Berdan Pan, used to crush very rich quartz; a Vibrating Concentrating Table, used to separate fine material containing gold from the tailings or waste; and an Amalgam Barrel in which gold is combined with mercury, separating it from waste material.

GOLD SMELTING WORKS

The Gold Smelting Works resembles one of the Quartz Mine's out-buildings. The Smelting Works contains an auditorium where visitors witness the final, dramatic stage in the story of gold – the smelting and pouring of liquid gold into a bar valued today at around $50,000. This demonstration includes information about the history of Ballarat's gold.

Visitors also have the opportunity to see a fully-restored 19th century coin press in action. Donated by Stokes of Melbourne, this magnificent press was originally used in the business established by Thomas Stokes, who came to Australia in the Gold Rush. In the Smelting Works, visitors may purchase an engraved souvenir medallion presented in a hand-crafted timber case. Gold nuggets and flakes of gold from Australian goldfields are also available.

UNDERGROUND DISPLAYS

Beneath the surface installations of the Sovereign Quartz Mine lies
a unique mining exhibit. By joining a fully-guided mine tour group,
visitors can walk through a series of long tunnels, or drives, to hear
stories of early mining and experience the feeling of working in an
underground mine. Along these drives, fascinating displays illustrate
quartz mining in Ballarat from 1860 to 1916 and depict the
technological development of the mining industry. The Beam Pump can
be seen in action underground, and there are original shafts and stopes,
excavated by miners on this site long before Sovereign Hill occupied it.
Visitors can also see the type of quartz reef that these miners were
searching for.

MINE TOURS

To take a fully-guided tour of the Quartz Mine's underground displays,
visitors should descend the steps at the hut near the Poppet Head. There
is also an alternative path, across flat ground, to the Mine. This path is
more suited to visitors with prams or wheelchairs. It starts from the
Diggings, behind the Temple in the Chinese Village. Mine tours are
available at regular intervals and take about forty minutes. Tickets must
be obtained at the Mine entry, as numbers per group are limited. The
tour exits from a track just above the entry point.

THE SECRET CHAMBER

Hidden deep within the Quartz Mine is *The Secret Chamber*. This
exciting exhibit is a state-of-the-art audio-visual presentation. It uses
breathtaking special effects to dramatise the story of two Chinese
brothers whose experiences typify the lives of some 10,000 Chinese
diggers who sought their fortunes in Ballarat during the 1850s Gold
Rush. The show takes ten minutes and is presented in Mandarin and
Cantonese Chinese, as well as English. It is available for group tours and
as part of the *Chinese on the Goldfields* tour.

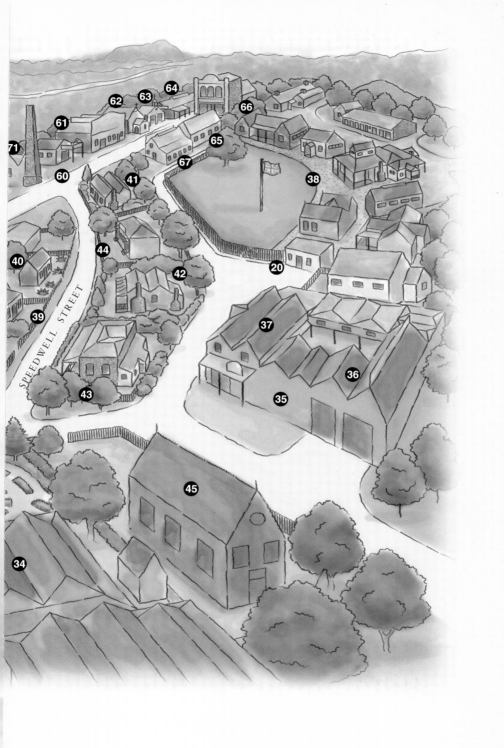

SPEEDWELL STREET